Can you ke

Can you keep a secret?

Jim Howes

Illustrated by Rae Dale

Addison Wesley Longman
Edinburge Gate
Burnt Mill
Harlow
Essex
CM20 2JE

© Addison Wesley Longman Limited 1997
This Edition of *Super Doopers* (First Edition)
is published by arrangement with
Addison Wesley Longman Australia Pty Limited,
South Melbourne, Australia
Second impression 1998

Copyright © text, Jim Howes, 1996
Copyright © illustrations, Rae Dale, 1996

All rights reserved. No part of this publication may be
reproduced, stored in a retrieval system or transmitted in any
form or by any means, electronic, mechanical, photocopying,
recording or otherwise, without the prior written permission of
the Publishers or licence permitted restricted copying in the
United Kingdom issued by the Copyright, Licensing Agency Ltd,
90 Tottenham Court Road, London, WIP 9HE

Project commissioned and managed by
Lorraine Bambrough-Kelly, The Writer's Style
Cover and text designed by Marta White

Set in Plantin
Produced by Addison Wesley Longman China Limited
GCC/02

ISBN 0 582 37657 2

The publisher's policy is to use paper manufactured from
sustainable forests.

'That's it,' shouted Sam as he came through the door. 'I've had enough!'

Sam's friend and fellow mouse, Wilfred, looked up from the cake he was making. His friend was very upset.

'Just look at me,' Sam went on.
'My tail was run over by a kid on rollerblades.

My coat was splashed by a lorry driving through a puddle of greasy gloop.

Drivers were throwing their rubbish out of the car windows as they passed. I was nearly bombed three times.

And when I jumped to dodge one missile, I stepped in something that is slowly melting my shoe.

And all I wanted was a quiet walk to the alley for a bit of supper.'

Sam opened the door again and pointed outside.
'Have you taken a good look at where we live
lately, Wilf?' he asked.

'It's noisier than a cat's wedding, messier than the bottom of a compost bin, more crowded than a free cheese festival and the air is the colour of egg yolk.

'I want to move.'

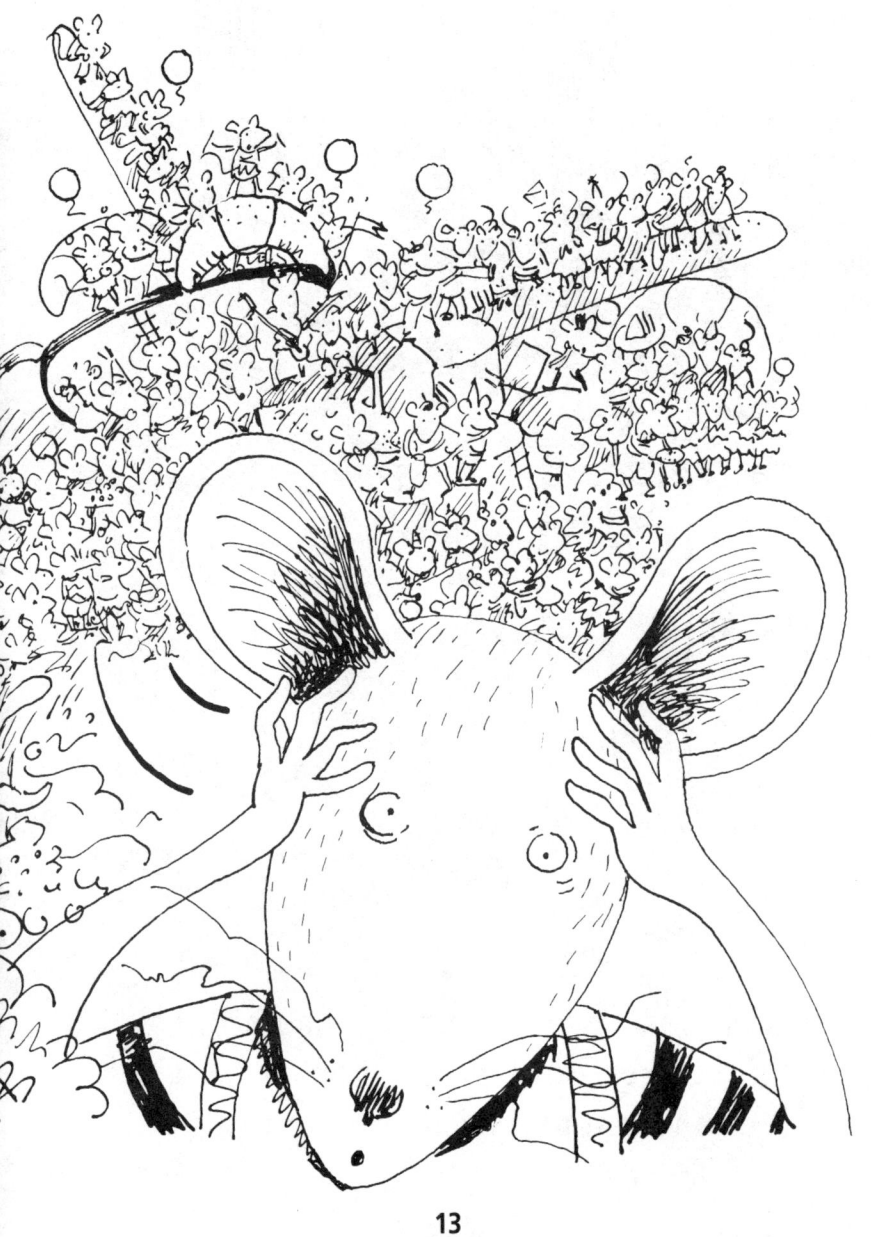

Wilf took a deep breath. He had heard all this before. 'But I *like* our house,' he said. 'I don't want to move.'

'Okay,' said Sam. 'You stay. But I'm going somewhere I can walk without my feet sticking to the ground and where I can breathe deeply without coughing.'

That very afternoon Sam packed his bag.
'Goodbye Wilf,' he said at the door. 'If I find a place, I'll write and let you know where to come and visit me.'

'That would be nice,' mumbled Wilf. 'I don't mind this place. I'll miss you, but you have to be where you are happy, Sam.'

With a hug, a handshake and a waving of their tails, the two friends parted.

Sam walked for five days and five nights before he was out of the city.

He walked for another five days and five nights before he was clear of the farms.

On the eleventh night he arrived at a small pool in a forest.

He stood still and listened. Silence.

He took a deep breath. Wonderful.

'This will do,' he told himself and crept under a small log to sleep.

In the morning Sam explored his new home.
He followed a short trail around the small pool.

Then he walked along a path that led around a bigger pool. There were fresh berries and mushrooms for breakfast. The water was cold and clear on his tongue. The ground was covered in lots of soft leaves and twigs.

'Ideal for building a home,' Sam said out loud. The place was perfect. It had everything he wanted. 'How could Wilf not come here and live with me?' he asked himself.

In no time at all Sam had made himself a home.
He built it with enough room for two, just in case.

That night he wrote his friend a letter and then posted it.

Dear Wilf
I have found a wonderful place to live.
I cannot begin to describe how beautiful it is.
Everything is clean and sparkling and the
songs of the other animals are a wonderful
change from the sound of machinery.
Please come and visit me here.
I know you will want to stay.

Your pal,
Sam

P.S. This is a map of how to find me.
I will start looking for you on the road on
the twelfth day.

Your pal again,
still Sam.

The next day Sam set about making the home as comfortable as possible.

He spent five days fixing up the house.

He spent another five making a small garden.

On the eleventh day he sat on the front step.

'If Wilf's coming he will be on his way now. He should be here tomorrow if he left when my letter arrived.'

He looked around. 'I think everything is ready. All I have to do is let Wilf see it for himself. I know he will love it.'

Then a small worrying thought crept into Sam's mind. 'What if he doesn't think it is beautiful?' he asked himself. 'I have to make sure that he sees everything at its best.'

With that, Sam dived into the house and started rummaging in the small box he had carried with him from the city. It was full of his toys and lots of shiny things he called his treasures.

Sam headed out along the path that led around the small pool. 'Maybe I should give nature a bit of help,' he said.

When he came to a large rock, he sprinkled some sparkles on it so it would glitter in the sunlight.

He climbed into the tree and hid his wind-up plastic bird. 'I hope it is still making a chirping noise when Wilf walks past,' said Sam.

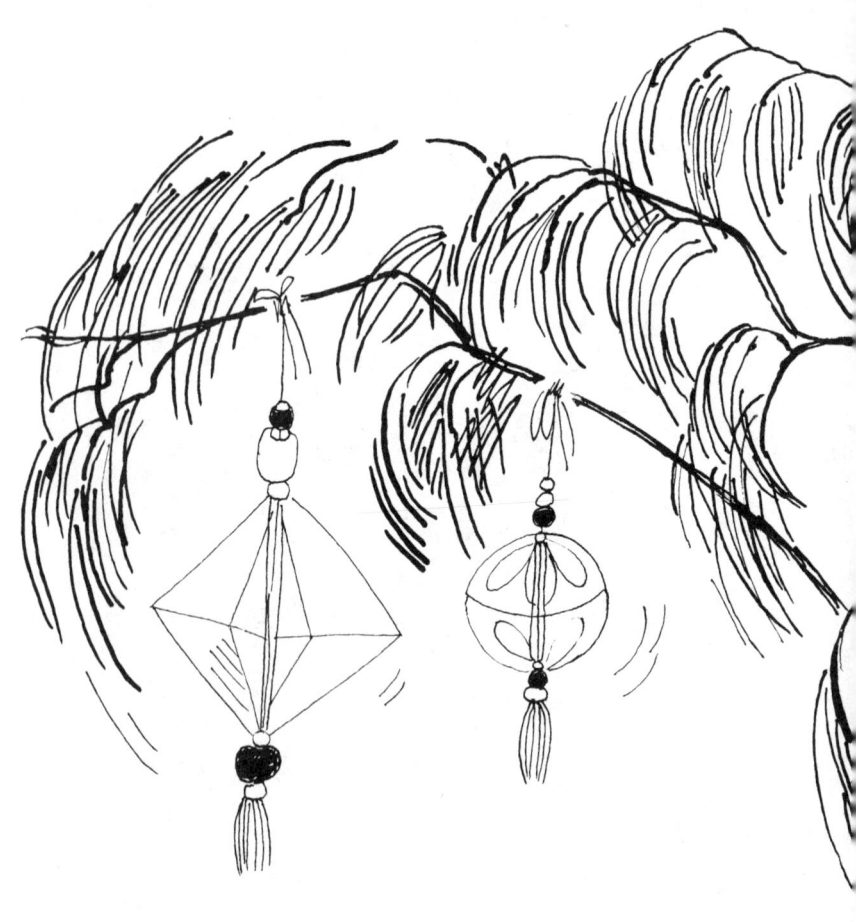

In another tree Sam hung a couple of glass baubles. 'These will glisten in the morning light like jewellery,' he said.

Sam went right around the pool and decorated the forest with his treasures and toys.

By the time he had finished, the forest by the path was filled with glittering objects and little toys that made small musical sounds.

Sam admired his work. 'Now Wilf is sure to like this place as much as I do and will want to stay,' he said, and headed home.

As he waited, Sam thought about his plan.
'Oh, I hope it works,' he muttered to himself.

'Who are you talking to, you mad mouse?' called a voice behind him. 'I leave you alone for a couple of weeks and you're already talking to the trees. I can see I came just in time.'

Sam spun around. There stood Wilf.
'Okay,' he laughed. 'I've tramped all the way out here. Show me your wonderful forest.'

Sam was glad to see his friend. He was also nervous about the things he had put in the forest and whether or not Wilf would like the place enough to stay.

'Before you sit down you must see it for yourself,' babbled Sam nervously.

'The morning is the best time. Now. Go now. I'll wait here and make some breakfast.'

Wilf was a little startled by Sam's pushiness but he agreed to go. 'Just head towards the pool, the small one,' called Sam as Wilf strolled off.

Sam went inside to make breakfast. Laying out his secret plan in the forest had made him hungry.

'I hope that little bird is still singing,' he whispered to himself.

Wilf walked slowly away from the little house.
He looked to the left and to the right for a pool.

And he found one on the right and another on the left. 'Which pool did he say it was?' wondered Wilf. 'Probably the big one.' And so Wilf headed down the path that led around the big pool instead of the smaller one where Sam had laid all his treasures. Sam's secret would be all for nothing.

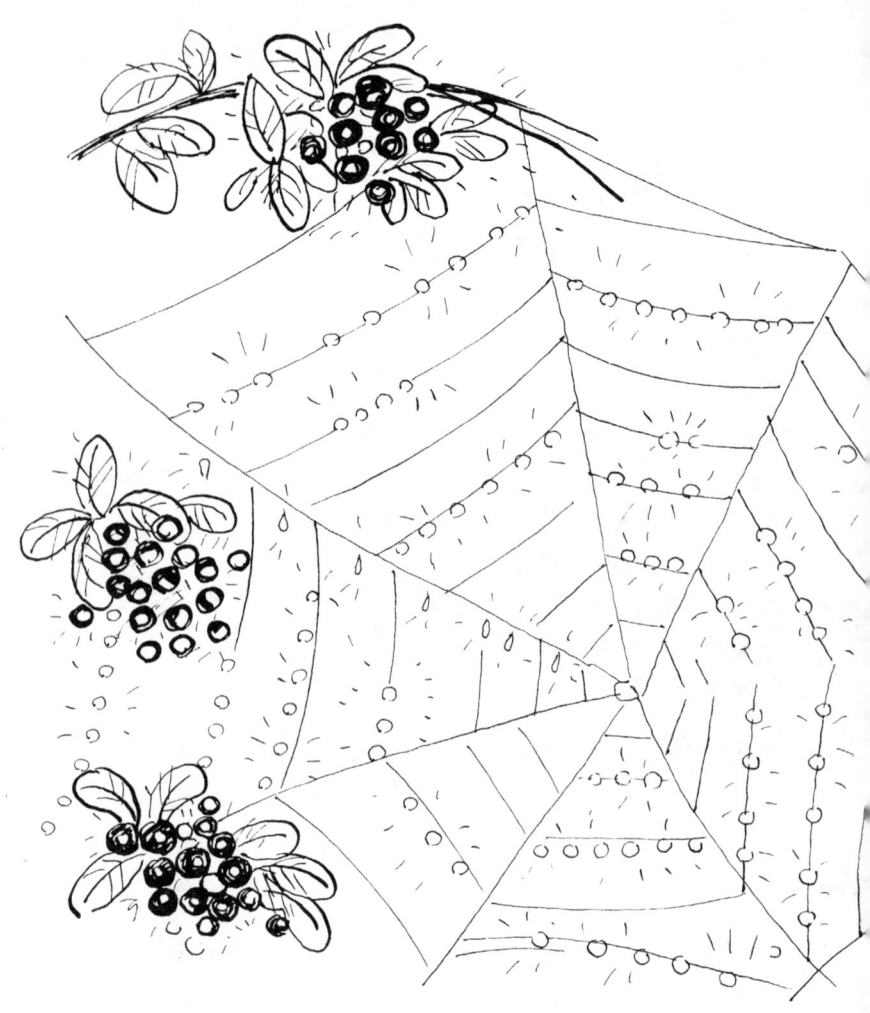

As he walked, he saw the light glistening on a dewy spider's web. There were coloured berries that shone like Christmas lights in the morning sun.

Two birds were competing with each other in song over his head. He was surrounded by colour and song.

When he returned to the house, Sam was
sitting on the front step with their breakfast.
He seemed nervous.

He watched Wilf coming towards him.
He tried to guess what his friend was thinking.
He wondered if his secret had been discovered.

Wilf sat beside him. Sam passed him a drink. Nobody said a word for what seemed like a lifetime to Sam. They just sat there. Sam was thinking about the decorations in the forest around the small pool. He hoped they had done their trick.

Wilf was thinking about all the things he had seen and heard as he walked around the big pool. He took a deep breath and sighed, 'This place is beautiful. I think I'd like to live here.'

'Good,' said Sam excitedly. 'I knew you would like it.'

Nobody spoke again for a long time.

Can *you* keep a secret?